50 Reasons
Not to Go Home for the Holidays

50 Reasons
Not to Go Home for the Holidays

Monica Sheehan and Tina Klem

**Andrews McMeel
Publishing**

Kansas City

Library of Congress Catalog Card Number: 97-71621

ISBN: 0-8362-3618-1

ATTENTION: SCHOOLS AND BUSINESSES

Andrews McMeel books are available at quantity discounts with bulk purchase for educational, business, or sales promotional use. For information, please write to: Special Sales Department, Andrews McMeel Publishing, 4520 Main Street, Kansas City, Missouri 64111.

To the 12 reasons to go home for the holidays:

my brothers and sisters—Michael, Stephen, John, Andrew, Peter, Sarah,

Nora, Ann, Tim, George, and Mary Jane;

and the most important reason of all: Mom.

—Monica

To my parents, who always seem to find a reason for bringing us together,

and to Aunt Fran, who always seems to be there.

—Tina

Acknowledgments

We would like to thank Rick Hill for putting up with our many reasons, and Gerry, Johnny, and Tim for their 50 words of support.

1. You have to leave your cat behind.

2. The dog's welcome is warmer than your family's.

3. Your childhood bedroom is now the home office.

4. Your grandmother thinks you look better with "a few extra pounds."

5. Your parents' "Christmas collection."

6. Your Aunt Elenore wants to know why you're not married.

7. Your mother forgot where she hid the silver.

8. Your father insists he got the best tree on the lot.

9. The cheese ball.

10. Your father asks your "new boyfriend" to help test the lights.

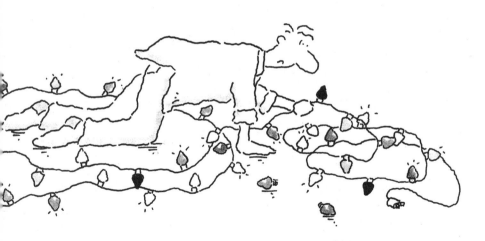

11. Your brother might have a job.

12. There's never enough Scotch tape.

13. Your sister's baby is still colicky.

14. You still have to sit at the kids' table.

15. You have to hear how great your cousins are doing.

16. The dinner conversation inevitably turns to "your job search."

17. Your Aunt Elenore wants to know why you're not married.

18. Everyone ends up in the kitchen.

19. Your parents still don't know how to work the VCR.

20. You still can't use the guest towels.

21. You have to sleep in separate bedrooms.

22. Your sister thinks you should live at home.

23. You become convinced that you don't have a life.

24. Your Aunt Elenore wants to know why you're not married.

25. You still can't take a shower when the dishwasher is running.

26. Your niece thinks you're the oldest in the family.

27. Your nephew thinks your new suede skirt is his blanky.

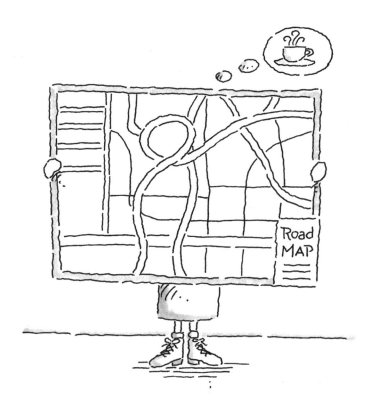

28. There isn't a caffè latte for twenty miles.

29. Your parents still buy in bulk.

30. Your mother wants to finish the vacuuming before 9:00 Mass.

31. Your neighbor, who is cat-sitting for you, can't find the keys to your apartment.

32. Your grandfather knows all the verses to "O Holy Night."

33. Mrs. Haloran is dropping off her infamous fruitcake.

34. Your nephew pulled your name out of the hat.

35. Your family claps after opening every present.

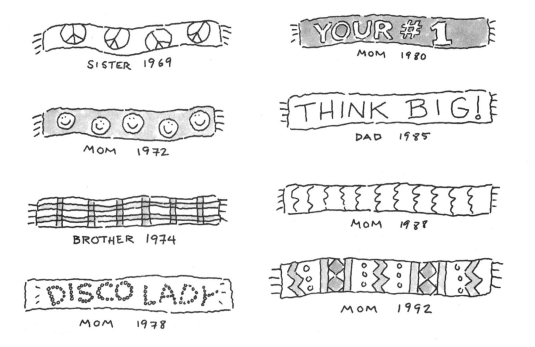

SISTER 1969

MOM 1972

BROTHER 1974

DISCO LADY
MOM 1978

YOUR #1
MOM 1980

THINK BIG!
DAD 1985

MOM 1988

MOM 1992

36. You can never have too many scarves.

37. Your mother thinks you can still "grow into it."

38. Your father needs a larger size.

39. You already have three Dustbusters.

40. Your mother found you a coat "very similar" to the one you asked for.

41. Your grandmother wants to save all the wrapping paper.

42. You still have to sneak cigarettes in the laundry room.

43. Your mother still believes she can do miraculous things with cream of mushroom soup.

44. There's never enough dark meat.

45. Your mother insists on you taking the rest of Aunt Helen's Jell-O salad.

46. Your Aunt Elenore wants to know why you're not married.

47. Everyone is too tired to drive you to the airport.

48. You realize a phone call would have sufficed.

49. You thought two hours a week of therapy was enough.

50. You thought this year would be different than the last.

Wrong!

About the Authors

Monica Sheehan and **Tina Klem** are childhood friends who met at the Blue Table in kindergarten. Their joint successes include first prize in their grade school science fair as well as numerous gold stars for their illustrated short stories in seventh and eighth grade English. Both Monica and Tina reside in New Jersey, pursuing careers in illustration, design, and Life 101. They each have two pet goldfish and a boyfriend.